Life's Reality Poetry

Georges Creations

A Collection of Poetry and Prose Poems

Volume I

Copyright © 2016 by Georges Creations

All rights Reserved. No part of this book may be reproduced Or transmitted in any form or by any means, without permission In writing from the publisher.

ISBN:978-0-6926-7274-7

Printed in the United States of America

ACKNOWLEDGEMENTS

I thank God almighty, for keeping me well and alive.

To my dear MOTHER, for always being there for me,
and being the source of my strength, besides the Lord.

To my late father, who would have enjoyed this book,
I miss you...

I would like to give special thanks to my dear aunt Gigi
My uncle Max & wife, for their motivations and help.

Last but not least: I would like to thank Ms. Lorraine Davis,
for being there for me.
Also to Martine Guiteau, and my friends who still believe in me.

God Bless You All!

CONTENTS

Rain   3
Reaching Deep   5
Thirsty For Red Miles Horses   6
Get the Fairness in Them   7
Unjust Plays   8
The Lost Boy   10
The Inside Song   11
Human Flaws   13
The Walk to All Destinations   15
Drum   17
Inner Demons   19
The Greedy   21
Conflicted Change   22
Lack of Happiness   23
The Crisis   24
Jesus of Nazareth   25
The Evangelist   28
Cutting Deep   30
Eyes Wide Open   32
Spiritual Voice   34
Can't Find the Way   35
Off Balance   36
A Pinch of Salt   37
The Game   38
A Fresh Breath of Life   39
Through These Lenses   40
Rock Bottom   41
Reaching 7 Heavens   42
Succulent Sour Taste (Headlines)   43
It Flows Through the Veins   44
The Unborn   46
Grey Surface   47
Life's Soldier   49
Sincerely With No Love   50

Rain!

Rain!

My scalp is dry
Blood clots throughout my veins, crossing my skull
Another desiccating day,
Is reaching my soul to subjugate my well-being,
Deserted is my path.

Rain!

My heart is beating like drums
From the cradle of civilization.
My vital force is crying out loud through miles universe,
My eyes are widely captured by the stars but shut.

The day is deranged and dried
The sun seared the soil, trees, and scorched the plains.
Nature is resting from erosion.

Animals are searching for constituents
Earth, fire, and the wind are desirous for water.
The sky losing its blue.

Rain!

Men and women are in extremis from dehydration
Exclaiming to the gods,
And yearning for life's serum.

The universe is striking bad energy
Desperate men are singing to the gods.
Fear of men mutating into beast,
Foreboding to undergo a replicate of the first temptation.

REACHING DEEP

The voice of self-conscious is raising its tone louder
to fight injustice, bias, and bullying among victims.

    Star of the Frenzied Show was booed
he couldn't entertain nor make anyone ecstatic,
due to his odious habits and inner demons are taking over.

    The Lion Monarchy Prince old ways
and crimes couldn't evoke, by his traumatized victims,
and his X factor Protégé/Preacher
is acting as congregation's leader.

    Fanatic Protestants were fasting till
collapsed on the hard surface,
they felt cogent to evince new members their tenacities,
on organized religion and supporting beliefs.

    The former leader of the Millennium March X is protesting
against bias and surviving the hard race,
engineered by subhuman architects of the planet Y.
No mercy under the subhuman regime.

    Poet of many verses has unleashed his true paradox
in which emphasized the mind child prisoner,
will stifle if not being removed inside the locked box,
so is the mind slave prisoner.

Thirsty For Red Miles Horses

Quenching on all there is
Thirsty for the serum of life's best.
Among the horses racing miles,
Competing fiercely to past all life's test,
To reach the finish line.
Due to bets are on the line.
The town's big money makers got bloody tough
On betting and will do what's vital,
To strive even to get undaunted and ruthless
On the riders & horses, to deliver for their sakes,
Till get deadly worn out and drop.
Even if they get destroyed after the finish line.
With eyes on the best horses,
And pressure on the equestrians
The biggest wagers were on the line between the kingpins
And the local politicians.
Their ways on monopolizing, subduing
And their hogging practices, have caused loathsome
Among some equestrians who are being coached to play devious,
Get ferocious, and to do whatever it takes to win.

Get the Fairness in Them

Half way down the sea
Are the young guns from the Law Centre,
Attempting to swim in with big fish and sharks,
To push for a new plea on the falsely accused man.
Fear of him divulging crucial secrets
While he was an inside man for the man.

The circuit judge is fed up
With sharks of the court,
Who brainwashed & maneuvered the jury
To an unfair plea against the unfairly accused.
Pushing for incarceration.

The headliners contrive to vex the vets
Which are ready to blow, aiming at the mockingbirds
Who are acting demented as a ruse to amuse,
And showing support to the jury cogent for conspiracy,
And obstruction of justice.
The case was transferred to a higher court.

UNJUST PLAYS

"TURN IT OFF, AND SHRUG OFF."

MODUS OPERANDI OF THE MASTERMIND
DESIGNING GRASPING PLOYS
PUSHING THE ENVELOP,
AND REIGN OVER.

SONS OF ABSORBED & WICKED KINGS
WERE MANIFESTING COVETOUS WAYS
AND PLAYING WITH HOT FIRE FOR ATTENTION,
NO TREPIDATION FOR THIRD-DEGREE BURN.
NEVERTHELESS, THEY CONTINUE
THEIR FARCICAL WAYS.

EQUITABLE FANS FROM THE CLEMENCY VILLAGE
ARE DISCERNING UNSPORTSMANLIKE CONDUCT,
FROM THEIR HOME TEAM.
A STRATAGEM FOR TRIUMPH, STRESSED BY THE TEAM
OWNERS.

CELEBRATING A BIG WIN, THEY WERE CHEERING
BY THE STEET GANGS,
DANCING TO SONGS OF MODERN DEVIL DISCIPLES
TO BEDEVIL PATHWAYS FOR GUEST PLAYERS,
AND TO KEEP THEIR BELLICOSE MOMENTUM.

THE UNJUST PLAYERS & HALFWITS
ARE SPECIALIZED IN PSYCHOLOGICAL EGOISM,
GRADUATED WITH HONORS,
AND PRIDE, BUT NO SUBSTANCE.

The Lost Boy

Searching for a soul, a childhood
Searching for joy and the boy within.
A lost childhood surviving mockeries, playing in the sun
in a pale skin, covering with mud to escape from anguish, prejudice
imploring for fun and peace, never a gun.

His mind, body and soul are eager for toxic cleansing.
He has gone a long way never cried a river,
and was liberated from unwanted colors, scars, glazes
inner pain and superfluous textures.

Brand new day,
brightens the sun transforms a smiley face,
to wide planet earth.
Birds are singing the song of the day.
Blood flows through his veins, new life within,
smiling till dawn. Treasure found within.

THE INSIDE SONG

    The sound engineer upraised the stakes higher
Strengthen the artist's inner voice who sung on no concept,
    And underperformed during a concert for destitute children.

    Nevertheless the ignoramus ostensible rising star
Is putting together a contest show for best singing lyrics,
For the mute and the deaf.

    Whereas the corner homeless blind man is dying to sing,
And listen to best Christmas album of the year.
He refuted on visualizing Santa's Elves,
Dancing on earth with human wolves.

    Surviving traumatic blows from reaching one's animal instinct
To battle deadly sea creatures due to smell of fear miles away,
From the captain of the phantom ship, who is addicted to mayhem.
Must stop playing devil's advocate.

  Allotting inner voice to good use
Outspoken vs radicalism are walking the line,
Democracy wins over.

  Extremism wants to dance the night away
With radicalism, uproar for freedom of speech,
And beliefs without rationale. Aspired to abuse democracy
And destroy a civilized society.

  The old conductor from the suburbs is fed up
With the same old musical notes, and the residents vile habits.
That inspired the new conductor of the elite orchestra,
He modified the rhythms, into genuine music to feed the soul.

The elite residents felt left out, betrayed, and walked out.

Human Flaws

A breath from the creator
an art of existence,
reaching out the world,
stressing elements of nature.
An obscure voice sings throughout thousands of miles away
from the soul,
embraces the universe becoming one.

Feeding into the roots of civilization
diffusing good and bad habits.
Fighting elements of nature and mankind.
A Necessary being is spoken,
searching for a purpose,
searching for lights and life.

Battle for power in the forest of tall trees.
Everybody wants to stand tall, to be king of the jungle,
King of the world and the universe.
A pattern of flaws and innate behavior,
overshadowing rationality,
challenging society and civilization.

Challenging nature and the Supreme Being
Inspire by evil forces of the gods and demons,
Hankering, grasping for power, and affluence.
Battles of civilizations,
still surviving the regime of mankind.

Newborn false prophets, displaying egocentric behaviors
Masquerading and pretense all.
Inadequacy to comprehend gender,
and see through true colors miles away
nor when birds fly with wings wide spread,
searching for nutriments.
New century king is born,
monopolizes the forest.

Different colors, texture preferences, yet same blood.
Spread of prejudice generates killings of roots
among the best trees.
Died of erosion, and contaminated substances,
Nonetheless fed to animals, destroyed by an evil Monarchy.
Time for harvest and new plantations,
new ways, new ruling, new life.
Revolution in the forest of survival.
We must survive.

The Walk to All Destinations

The unknown homeless man
Walks with a luggage of burden from dawn till dusk.
He wakes up to a new day and a new journey of despair.
Searching for life's destination, for water, sun and light.
He undergoes the inconceivable,
And absorbs the sour taste of life.
He surmounted the elements of nature
(Rain, sun, water and wind.)
Beaten by cold-blooded men, and Mother Nature's aggressive
And unpredictable ways.
The homeless man reads everyone he encounters within his path,
And each body language.
He's gifted with the ability to see and comprehends good & evil
From any forms, or shapes.
His sense of smell is sharper than a butcher knife.
The homeless man walks and walks, and walks,
Yet he doesn't succumb, nor shows any weary sigh.
He has no fear, and no hesitation to face life,
As if he mastered fate, and wisdom.
His body rest till birds rest,
Conversely, his mind is opposed to repose.

His thoughts travel day and night, miles away
Dance with ANGELS of mercy,
He has read the book of GOD and men.
He understands the bona fide philosophy of life and religion.
Yet The School of Hard Knocks.
The homeless man from nowhere,
Moves with confidence,
As if he knows all his destinations.
He carries his life's story around his hair, eyes,
Face, beard, walks, moves,
The grime layers of clothing he wears from everyday struggle,
Inside the multiple bags, he carries in his cart and around his shoulders,
Which contains personal items of every day's survival.
He has the strength of a king from the jungle
And a beast.
He is short-spoken and possesses an intriguing mien of a SAINT.
He smiles in a glance motion. He looks down,
Up and deep inside primarily at society's scathing ways,
Mistreatment and misjudgment in which he was victimized by.
He refuses to be looked as a charity case,
Nor less than a human being.
He doesn't beg for any piece of change, nor accept any.
Everyone questions how does he survives or get by?
He's not sheltered by anyone, but the STREETS
And from above.
He's against any indulgence and prejudice.
Nor ever wanna be treated less than a man.

Drum

Beating miles away from the cradle of civilization
To the first race, the first king, and first queen.
Moving the human race,
Moving mankind singing out loud.

Singing to elements
Of the universe and men,
Expressing to nature,
Conveyed to Kings and Lords.

Drum
Awakens the human from the motherland
Its genesis, its essence,
And its existence.

Drum
Basic foundation, art of expression
Tool for combats, revolutions,
Fights, leaders of pathways.

Soul searching, independence
Battles, slavery, inequality, equality
Rights, injustice, justice,
Visions and freedom.

Drum
Original sound of a race,
The human race.
Music of authenticity and civilization.

From the cavemen to the slaves,
And the slaves to the Masters.
From Masters to the Kings,
From the Kings to the Lords,
The orient to the occident.

A universe of progressive society.

Inner Demons

Voices from inner self are skirmishing dark clouds
Swimming with deadly sharks, and the sea Queen
To reach destinations,
And fighting inner demons.

The abuse and addictions
Lost touch, out of reality
Living throughout space.

The anger and chaos
Playing fatal games of death,
Evil lyrics are deafeningly entertaining the brain,
Notwithstanding deaf.

Wars in the brain
One wants to scream through planets,
Dancing with dead stars, and invariably in pain.

Behaving irrational ascending steps, without heights
Nor destinations.
Hell with the suppliers of no conscience.
MERCENARIES and brain killers.

Eyes from the muddling mind reading invisible clocks,
At a black and white wall, no gray area.
Crossing a river swimming with ducks,
Hallucinating multiple colors with a new persona,
Becomes bipolar and travels in Luna.

Must cross new paths, new bridges.
Must kill the inner demons,
Or one will be killed,
By evil sermons in the brain.

The Greedy

Guzzling a full taste of life's best
Feeling powerful, and overindulged all.
Desserts of the best were served,
From the Master Chef,
Celebrating victory on blood money.
An impulse to covet for more turn anything into profits,
And agonizing others without compunction for ruined lives.
Crowned as King of Wall Street,
And proudly named natural born killer instinct to the core.
Skilled to obliterate anything for money, and for opulence.
Derided till cramping.
No conscience,
No heart,
No soul,
No worries. No regards. No rules. No mercy.
Relentless bloodsucking ways.
It's inhumane.

Conflicted Change

Inner change of new ways and new forms,
under the blue sky.

The born pilot is avoiding air conflicts,
among the lost destination mockingbirds.
He must fly in a no-fly zone.

Nature changes of plans, and paths.
Maliciousness and animal instinct of the walking dead,
unleashed outcomes, designed for wrong paths.

Force of circumstances and society's pressure,
erratic behavior and imploring for acquisitiveness, ensuing
fear of change, fear of being judged.

Lack of Happiness

From the stars to the mood of happiness
to the source of sweet life's water,
a thirst and tang for sweet happiness within.
The subconscious from one feeling happy
and the reality of awareness.
Feeling the great invisible elements of happiness.

Impairments of pessimism
thus, handicap rationality,
and lack of realism, must avoid a toxic mind.

The voice of happiness
nothing less,
hope for success and greatness.
Taste of succulent dessert of delicious sherbet,
toppings from the best for the best.

Weak foundations
And evil dance with lions,
aiming at innocent creatures,
Rekindled dried dead leaves into green leaves,
for wealth and power.
Guzzling blood champagne on Necessary
and Contingent beings as a substitute of real happiness,
is inhumane.

The Crisis

Same songs, playing broken records of hits
Trying for survival,
Not want to believe in myths.

The church bell is ringing for deliverance
And the parishioners are hoping for the marching band,
To play the music of hope, to lift their spirits.

The farmers are desperately invoking for rain
To water the new planted grains,
Attempting to stop the path of deadly erosion
And a déjà vu of crisis,
Which they were never surmounted.

JESUS of Nazareth

Our SAVIOR and KING

In dreams and reality save us from malefic men,

in the valley of death.

Don't let us succumb by the voracity,

and malice of walking human vultures,

be our protector and Shepherd.

Our LIGHT

Walk with us, brighten the pathways,

and shadow of darkness.

Open our eyes, and help us see the light from all.

Clear out our sorrows, deliver us from all sins,

and make it all right.

Our ROCK and Guidance

Let us lean on you,

and help us climb the mountain of uncertainty every day.

Give us strength, direction

and lead us to the best destination,

until we reach the final gate.

Our ARCHITECT

Build the best and most solid shelter

to protect ourselves from forces of nature,

and life's defect,

be our sentinel.

Our PROTECTOR

Protect us from bad spirits, vicious men,

evil, crimes, tragic accidents, and danger.

Help us be prudent,

make it better and safer.

Our LORD

Deliver us from all temptations

and adversities.

Give us devotions, perseverance, and peace.

Help us be human, not turning into a beast.

Our WAY and TRUTH

Inspire us to be the best,

To be true to ourselves and others.

To have faith in you,

and our holy father in heaven.

Give us the courage

And triumph to conquer all obstacles

and challenges we might face.

                            Amen!

The Evangelist

J. Doe, the dearest preacher in the suburb VII
Has unleashed his prominent paradox.
A well twisted and engineered sermon on church day,
To lure and proselytize visitors and parishioners.
It was acclaimed by the hardcore adherent Protestants,
Loyal church members and his protégés,
Who are indeed brainwashed?
Furthermore, ongoing conflicts on manifold interpretations
Of the BIBLE, unreasoned views, and the art of proselytizing secular
Into non-secular groups, (Organized religion) have joined forces.
No rules, no regards, no respect for ADONAI,
Nor for society.
No PRINCIPLE, but plenty of LIES and AUDACITY to induce.

Evangelist J. Doe, and other leaders from the non-secular group X
Have launched their best CRUSADE, yet on LUST, ADULTERY,
MONEY, POWER, HUMILITY, GIVING, POVERTY,
CHARITY, DOCTRINE, LEADING A DOUBLE LIFE,
ASCETICISM and CORRUPTION in the CHURCH.
Nonetheless FAILED to practice on what they PREACHED.
No COMPUNCTION on their part.

The darling evangelist is adept at
Possessing MINDS and BODIES.
He assured the new recruits of being saved and protected,
By the PAGAN church conducting by Reynard characters,
On the basis of personal gains, riches,
And use the Holy name of JEHOVAH in vain.
Barefaced behaviors.

Subsequent to a lavish lifestyle and leading a double life,
Furthermore to sustain the charade;
He designated his former dealer and associate as lead preacher,
To oversee his new church, that he built in the Z-town.
He reinforced and enhanced the methodology among
His parishioners, to exercise Bible-thumping.
Ergo, he recruited a team of women to inveigle.
He professed to keep the Protestantism movement alive,
Wherefore his team members were coached,
And appointed to exert the "WORD"
Maneuver and targeting innocent, susceptible minds.
"It's a way to catch new fish," he said.
No HEART. No MERCY.

The Saga Continues…

Cutting DEEP

The undefeated butcher of all MEAT
is slicing deep to the bones till crying blood.
From the tough skin, it's withstanding to DEFEAT.

Warning! No one can swim in the river of dead FISH,
Till sharks get a reality check. Stopping the bad chef
from making a pungent seafood DISH.

Changing the DYNAMICS,
among birds from flying high and speaking the ugly truth,
won't stop the nosy parrot to spill the beans and his MIMICS.

If one's losing track of the human RACE,
best getting oneself check before next destination,
to evade in an inapt PLACE.

Tears from feigned EMOTION,
filled up the baptism river for Protestants, whom cried a river,
to prove a point. No one shows regard or COMPASSION.

Inside one's WORLDVIEW,
feeling as the only human dwelling,
from a pattern of fighting rationality with a pessimist
VIEW.

    Turmoil and conflicts within self,
led to the walk with soldiers of ANARCHY,
one must not cross the line to affect LIBERTY.

    The general of evil regime,
is still spreading barbaric and wants to destroy DEMOCRACY.
An illicit pattern to destroy freedom,
in a civilize SOCIETY.

    The smell of fear and bad SPIRITS,
kindle the fierce creatures to misbehave,
and the underground city gangs,
which are crossing their lines, and LIMITS.

    Surviving brutal attacks
from goading the animal INSTINCT,
one must heal the scars of the true living.
No blood scattering to confuse as PINK.

    The Art of War among innocent DOVES,
is turning into bloodshed,
galvanized the fascist and his regime into killing all mockingbirds,
on the COVES.

Eyes Wide Open

    Catnapping with eyes widely open
The mind is scrutinizing miles away without awareness,
Nor compromise.

    Observing the big picture of oneself and Necessary Beings
Aspired to carry the torch of being ingenious as the great Dr. Max X,
Nevertheless repudiated image of the real Dean,
One must show reverence.

    Insinuating irrational judgment with naked eyes
Should remove self from judges seats,
Once out of the chamber.

    Must let better relevance and logic precept
Or principle fundamental, and rationality,
Will convert into chaos.

    Eyes of the mind and the brain
Prophesying future reality should remain plain.
Must not be in vain.

True colors being seeing
When weighting candidly at reality,
Not half way through sleep.

Recapitulating large volumes of unfair judgment
Prior the full perusal,
Bias rationality, not intellectually accurate.

Eyes open wide but shut
One should perceive genuine colors,
And regiments.

Real essence looking at the truth
Free from any radicals cells and color-blind,
For better judgment.

Spiritual Voice

Singing to souls, transform beast into human.
Singing to God and angels.
Reaching the foundation of all.
Healing wounds, stopping the bloodshed.

The power to heal the broken heart
And reconciles lost human relation.
Putting together pieces of lost puzzles,
Repair defective passion.

Touching millions
With the best instruments.
Changing lives deep inside.
Put the mind to rest and everything else aside.

The ability to cure
And heal the scars if survive,
Often may not be revivified.

Alternative of practical therapy
A potential way to survive best keynotes,
And inside music of the living,
Rouses the human spirit.

Can't Find The Way

Half way asleep in the lost forest
        birds are flying miles away,
         searching for a nest to rest.

Living phantoms of fictitious world,
        have shown directions to pathways in dreams,
        it was more frightened when awakened,
        observing children of men,
        hounding the weak and the innocent
Accentuating unnecessary wars and battles,
        over pointless justifications.

The ignoramuses engineers are designing
        a project in their city,
        with no substructure and eagerness.
        They were undaunted to swim with deadly sharks,
        to reach the top. In lieu of doing good vs evil.

The leader of the free radical cells from the beast
        has launched the strike of the century,
Aiming to kill the parrots and freedom of speech.

Off Balance

     Precarious limitation and locking inside the box
a mutual way as living with smallpox.

     The obdurate Prince of folly
is inadequate to see the light,
        pathways to brightness and interchange.

     Beautiful lady of the neighborhood of anarchy
     is seduced by the bystanders of chaos,
who fueled bad blood towards the youths to get angry,
and to disseminate violence.

     The girl next door is working on letting her hair down
on origin, race and views.
     She's finally figured out her race,
and the real texture of her skin which is brown.

Open oneself to learn the art of compromise
       dodging prophets of false promises,
       one won't fall into a counterfeit.

     Reality check within self
must not compromising,
       nor a pattern of self-denial.

     The former colonel from the deadly army
has finally put two and two together,
after he was ousted.

A Pinch of Salt

Tasteless, conflicted tongue,
    Swimming in saltless water.
    The captain is fishing in rough seas;
    Losing ability to swim along with the clever kings
    Of the river.

The mouth is confined inside its prison guard,
    What a waste! Mimicking songs of fake patriots,
    Hallucinating through an invisible wall.
    Longing for salted mixed,
    The result from the lack of real taste.
    Spreading buttery idiots joke over French toast,
Triggered the gang of lost soul and sense of tasteless.

    Can't avoid when it's time to get roasted,
    A little pinch smothered over the best,
    Save for last.
    No need to impel crossing turtles,
    May not enjoy a little taste of salt flavor,
    If quickening.

THE GAME

Playing life's poker
Victory wins over glory.
Contemptible conscience over triumph.

The fierce boys from the poker club
Hankering to recapitulate verses to dead poets,
Orchestrated with deadly themes, to scare.

The church bell is crying out loud to reach out lost souls,
Of the city due to loud malicious tunes,
From the punk musicians of lost planet X.

Good vs evil walk side by side
Satan's disciples have prepared their own last supper,
Dictating the human race, and hunger for absolute power.

Politics of beautiful speech
And sweet poems,
Exhilarating minds of the weak, and the innocent.

Virgins species took a walk on the moon,
Followed the lead of fake astronauts,
And dead stars. Led to nowhere.

The ruthless dictator has played his last desperate card
To stay in power,
Outcome of poor judgments, corruptions and crimes
Prompted to the fall of his empire, and an era. Game over!

A Fresh Breath of Life

Mother nature is scattering fresh breeze
breaths of life on living beings,
and communicating languages of roots to mankind.

The birds are flying on high altitude
coming down low to their niche full of grains,
singing songs of peace along with doves.

The sea is soothing
washing away invisible dirt of human soul,
allaying and preaching calamity to earth.

The sky modifies its blue to grey
making ways vaguely for indiscernible planes to soar,
until reach destinations to dwell.

Through These Lenses

The inquisitive eyes of one's mind foreseeing miles away
Color blind and behind walls.
One's eyes viewing elements with relish,
And fictionalized over butterflies.

The pedestrians in the crosswalk
Are taking steps ahead of the slow track,
To avoid chaos with the king X and lords of the block.

Rich kids from the conservative Christians neighborhood
Got into mischief, crossed a thin line between life and death,
Before being stopped by the vigilant watchman.

Through These Lenses
Observing the neighborhood watchdog,
Barking at invisible villains,
Smelling evil and danger from the critters.

One witnessed new scent from summer,
To autumn fallen leaves expressing mood swings.
Flaunting true colors of men desire for power,
Obsession to be adored, and walk over the weak.

Through These Lenses
Secrets between cat and mouse were finally leaked,
And disclosed.

Rock Bottom

The mind, body and soul are searching for peace
Not the least.
Battling self-being.

The inner voice is declaiming poems to lost souls
Angels vs demons are singing opera to phantoms,
Shed no tears to the fools.

Inner demons overshadowing one's reality
And rationality,
Irrationality seized the lead,
And reached the bottom of the barrel.
Attempted to taste the last pinch of salt,
And life's sugar flavor, but reached rock bottom.

The inner child of innocence is asphyxiated,
Due to spite, and pleonexia,
Are emerging in the *Vallée* ruling by Sons of Evil Men.
Victory vs no conscience.
Sucking on lemon, sitting on precious metals,
And dead presidents for opulence.

Reaching 7 heavens

One is reaching within 7 heavens
Experiencing the mood of space.
Discerning color and its true essence.

One's reaching 7 heavens

Fleeing reality, living in an abstract world,
From living prophets. Thus, become aware.
Desire to become own king and master of own craft,
The true Dean of the University of Common Sense.

One's reaching 7 heavens

Speaking the truth and wisdom,
On the microphone of bullshit less,
To the insensible audience.
Distinguishing within the inside man, and the inside job.
Putting the lost pieces together,
And resolve the puzzle on the dark surface.

Reaching 7 heavens

Eyes of the mind reflect a 20/20 vision
No need for new lenses.
Genuine eyes are exploring bona fide colors, and flaws.
The Awarded Artist of the New Millennium,
Is finally applying his skills and paint brush to good use,
On blank surface, without getting frightened
Of society's hypocrisy, favoritism and its criticism.

Succulent Sour Taste (Headlines)

1-
Main crops were served during a luncheon,
By the king farmer, from the hidebound township
To introduce his new harvests for supply and demand.
A beloved agronomist specialized in sugar cane
Had tried to refine the roots from amiss plantations,
To rectify the conservative township loathsome habits,
On resisting to virtue ethics, no good deeds,
And serving a sour taste of life to others.
Subsequently a nice garnishment of sea creatures,
From the upper class of the hills, arrayed at their formal dinner
Celebrated new ways on monopolizing the middle-class merchants.

2-
Surviving believers from the former cult X
Of the town's secret society, have joined the club of free spirit
Nullifidian, and switched to a phase of dullness.
Nonetheless, the new "Kid" on the block is promulgating his wings
Among the innocent youths,
Emphasizes his love for pasta and reinforcing old ferocious ways,
Of the former Godfather.

3-
The former convicted preacher of the United Sept of Followers
Asserted he found true salvation while incarcerated.
He wants to work his way to a new era of authentic Christianity,
And the philanthropist from the Giving Club vs Cupidity,
Won the year humanitarian award among the graduates,
From the township School of Greed & Art of Manipulations.

It Flows Through The Veins

Myths or reality of the mindset
Inducing reverse psychology and ludicrous,
From breaking bad habits of the crew,
Fallen from high altitude
Striking all vulnerable species,
And ruled overall.
Breaking bad among aggressive bears.
Engendered new king of animal dictatorship,
For generation X,
Live or die.

The captain of the Crew IX Ship
Wanted to turn the boat away,
Attributable dangerous invisible species
From the universe and the sea.
Along the way, he must fight the fisherman
Of the pirate gang, a proud king of strife,
To reach his destination.

Passengers ahead from the reality boat
Are dangerously playing life's poker to win the best prize,
Organized by secularists.

The former blues singer from The Hard Knocks Café
Is teaching the new lead singer real life's keynotes,
And fact-based blues from The University of Hard Knocks.

Loyal fans applauded and embraced the new hardcore tones,
They felt the glide within their veins and soul,
Asked for an ENCORE.

The Unborn

Inside her womb
Is growing the fruit of natural creation,
Her mind, body and soul unified the tone in one portion.
Inside her gray matter, is a flow of ardor
Crossing her soul, feeling a sense of grace.
She dances day and night, with her inside music
And regains her glide and the mood of true living.
Inwardly, genuinely and vaguely ignored critics.
Her body and soul opposing to aborting,
Nevertheless, her spirit determined to cross the line.
Wreaked is the bag carries her natural fruit of life.
Impassioned and tears,
Begin to water the planted dying seed of her wounds.
Vulnerability and mayhem dictated her well-being,
Took over her site,
Tempted for her knife.

Grey Surface

The painting artist of the year feels no mercy
on exposing the gray area to all surfaces,
applying true colors and life to the dead museum walls
and a new art exhibition, for the deluded public.

Inside man & director from the museum
of civilizations and false prophets,
felt threaten by the artist's bold move,
and riveting to protect hidden and grimy secrets from the museum.
He defies freedom of expression of any form or race.

Fans from the nationalist group
have shown support for the artist,
and to unseat the former general acting senator,
stressing to resurface Martial Law
and sparks loathing with the museum director.

Former boys band of baby boomers,
are pushing the envelope on free speech,
due to the new elected lawmaker is mandating new rules,
and manifesting discrimination on race and gender.

The local Disc Jockey has unleashed songs of freedom,
and equality to beseech volumes of true patriots,
to fight for human rights, until the records reach millions,
and go platinum.

The teacher from the school of unity,
and higher education, is battling idiocy and crimes
in her city.
Fear of bad sons of men
will corrupt the innocuous minds in her class.

Life's Soldier

From the early fights
To the rise of freedom,
Died of thirst in the desert of lost world
And bathing in mud.
A pale worn out uniform
With blood stains and colors of abuse,
Agony from men turned into subhuman.
Surviving the darkness moment,
Of the aftermath,
When dreams and family were raped,
By evil practices, and crimes on humanity.
From daily struggle within the snow-white,
And wolves patrons from the clans of avaricious sharks.
Revolving a pattern of stony-hearted, human destructors.
Killings of the productive, covenant,
And the hard working class producing the best of the best.
The life's soldier has survived all, and rose above all.

Sincerely With No Love

She walks her catwalk by moving her hips
    Laying her eggs over the emptiness of her nest.

I was staring at her beautiful lying violet render lips,
    Wondering the time she'll put them to rest.

    The eyes of her suspicious mind could tell a lie vividly
    Such talent she possesses if not her best.

Around her astonishing outfit flowing layers rapidly.
    The seduction of her body is fierce as a pest.

    The soft sexy sound of her tone targets electrons in the brain,
Deep inside the sense of hearing.

    The music she sings is as good as it gets, not in vain.
    And did I mention she was bloody sexually daring?

Love

Peace

And

Harmony

GOD Is LOVE

Deus Amor Est

www.ingramcontent.com/pod-product-compliance
Lightning Source LLC
Chambersburg PA
CBHW020023050426
42450CB00005B/620